ID0407803

# The
# World Trade
# Center
# Bombing

Titles in the *American Disasters* series:

# The Exxon Valdez
## Tragic Oil Spill
ISBN 0-7660-1058-9

# Hurricane Andrew
## Nature's Rage
ISBN 0-7660-1057-0

# The Oklahoma City Bombing
## Terror in the Heartland
ISBN 0-7660-1061-9

# Plains Outbreak Tornadoes
## Killer Twisters
ISBN 0-7660-1059-7

# San Francisco Earthquake, 1989
## Death and Destruction
ISBN 0-7660-1060-0

# The World Trade Center Bombing
## Terror in the Towers
ISBN 0-7660-1056-2

# The
# World Trade
# Center
# Bombing
## Terror in the Towers

Victoria Sherrow

 **Enslow Publishers, Inc.**

44 Fadem Road           PO Box 38
Box 699               Aldershot
Springfield, NJ 07081   Hants GU12 6BP
USA                         UK

**Library of Congress Cataloging-in-Publication Data**

Sherrow, Victoria.
The World Trade Center bombing : terror in the towers / Victoria Sherrow.
     p. cm. — (American disasters)
    Includes bibliographical references and index.
    Summary: Details the events surrounding the 1993 bombing of the
World Trade Center as well as the investigation and trial of those
responsible for the terrorist attack.
    ISBN 0-7660-1056-2
    1. World Trade Center Bombing, New York, N.Y., 1993—Juvenile
literature. 2. Terrorism—New York (State)—New York—Juvenile literature.
3. Bombing investigation—New York (State)—New York—Juvenile literature.
[1. World Trade Center Bombing, New York, N.Y., 1993. 2. Terrorism.
3. Bombing investigation.] I. Title. II. Series.
HV6432.S54   1998
364.1'09747'1—dc21                97-45769
                                      CIP
                                      AC

Printed in the United States of America.

10 9 8 7 6 5 4 3 2 1

**Photo Credits:** AP/Wide World Photos, pp. 1, 6, 8, 10, 13, 15, 16, 17, 18, 21,
22, 23, 24, 26, 28, 32, 34, 35, 38, 40, 41.

**Cover Photo:** AP/Wide World Photos

# Contents

CHAPTER **1**

# A Nightmare We All Went Through

It was February 26, 1993, around midday—12:18 P.M. to be exact. About fifty thousand people were inside the World Trade Center building in New York City. The center's 110-story twin towers are the tallest buildings in this bustling city. They house more than three hundred different businesses.

Each morning, tens of thousands of people arrive to work in the towers. Others come and go to deliver supplies or mail. Salespeople come to meet with their clients. Still other workers repair and maintain this huge structure.

The towers also attract many tourists. On this snowy day, hundreds of schoolchildren and their teachers were visiting. They had taken elevators to the top of the skyscraper. From there, they gazed down at the awesome view of New York.

People throughout the towers were going about their business. It seemed like any other Friday. But these people were in for the shock of their lives. A huge explosion was about to erupt beneath them. It would wreak havoc in the towers and change their world.

Artie Zanfini, a manager at the Nynex Business Marketing organization, was on the thirteenth floor that day. He recalls, "You heard a very loud sound—it's hard to describe. It sounded like a loud rush of air. All the lights went out."[1] Nobody knew for sure what had happened. "But you knew *something* was seriously wrong," says Zanfini.[2]

Tom Failand, an elevator usher, was on one of the top

A police officer and a security officer direct traffic as people rush from the World Trade Center after the bomb blast.

floors at 12:18 P.M. He remembers, "The lights went out. Then the smoke came. And then we went up to the roof, and we ended up there for quite a few hours."[3]

Seventy-two people were caught inside one of the elevators. One man describes his experience: "BOOM! Suddenly the elevator screeched to an abrupt halt. . . . Then there was another 'click' and everything went black, not just dark but pitch black."[4] This elevator remained stuck between floors for hours. Trapped inside were many schoolchildren. They waited fearfully in the dark. Some held hands. Many could not hold back their tears.

Standing in the smoke and darkness, people wondered what could have happened. What had made those awful booming noises? Was the smoke evidence of a deadly fire? Why didn't the lights come back on?

Anthony Short, of the Port Authority of New York and New Jersey was among those who would never forget this day. Later, Short would call the World Trade Center bombing "a nightmare that we all went through."[5]

# CHAPTER 2

# Hours of Confusion

**A**fter the explosion, people inside the towers dialed emergency phone numbers. There was no answer. By now, sirens were wailing outside the building. Emergency vehicles screeched to a halt on the streets.

People in the World Trade Center still had no idea what had happened. What should they do? Should they stay put or try to get downstairs? Artie Zanfini and his group at Nynex decided to leave the building. The power was out, so all the elevators were dead. This group of about two hundred people hurried toward the stairs. They began the long trip down on foot. Zanfini recalls, "The stairwells were rapidly filling with black, sooty smoke. But we got out in an orderly way."[1]

Lisa Vasquez, a secretary for the Dean Witter stock brokerage firm, worked on the sixth floor. She described the scene as they walked out: "The smoke was coming and we were inhaling it and people coughing and trying to hurry up and get out. . . ."[2]

Other people also escaped soon after the blast. Many were stuck inside narrow, smoke-filled stairways, stalled elevators, or other places. Some victims had been injured by the blast. They had been hit and cut by pieces of debris. Others had fallen in the darkness or fainted from inhaling smoke. These victims worried when—and if—help would come.

Out in the streets, crowds were gathering. They stared at the smoking towers. Police directed traffic and worked to keep order. They cleared the way as medics hurried to the scene. They gave victims first aid. People with serious injuries or health problems were rushed to hospitals.

The hours after the bombing were hectic. Medics and ambulances kept busy as more injured people came out of the towers. They were suffering from smoke inhalation or shock. Some victims complained of back and neck pain. Many said they heard a ringing sound in their ears.

Victims who had been near the lower levels of the towers suffered from the worst injuries. Those who could not walk, or who seemed to have head or back injuries, were placed on stretchers. A few people suffered heart attacks.

Within three hours, two hundred people were brought to the emergency room of New York Downtown Hospital. The hospital was not equipped to handle so many injured patients. Doctors and nurses worked at top speed. They focused on the most urgent cases. The hospital ran short of heart and lung equipment. By day's end, a total of one thousand people were reported injured.

Back inside the towers, many people were still

ork City firefighters break windows at the
Trade Center to vent some of the smoke after
ry explosion.

trapped. More than one hundred kindergarten children waited for hours inside dark elevators. Their teachers later told reporters that the children passed some of the time snacking on milk and cookies. But as the hours dragged by, the children became upset. One teacher said they were "a little scared" and wanted their mothers. Some prayed.[3]

One of the seventy-two people trapped in one elevator recalled the long wait. It took more than four hours before anybody spoke to them over the speaker inside the elevator. When no help came, he said, "[the children] started to cling to the adults in sheer fright. Kids couldn't stop crying. Parents couldn't stop ranting and complaining. I could no longer tune it out."[4]

At last, firefighters came to the rescue. They used sledgehammers and picks to break through the wall above the elevator. One tourist recalled:

> No sooner had we started to get a few out, when the elevator jolted and began accelerating downward! Not a freefall, thank God, but fast enough that everything whizzing by was merely a blur. As we slowed to a stop, the kids cheered and giggled. The rest of us sighed in relief.[5]

They finally reached the sidewalk safely. There they saw crowds of people, reporters, TV cameras, police, and ambulances. Tom Failand and his fellow elevator ushers were also rescued late that afternoon. They could finally come down from the top of the tower. Failand remembers, "We walked down the 110 flights of stairs."[6]

In all, it took six hours before everyone was rescued from the towers. Rescuers battled thick smoke and the lack of electrical power. They had to move carefully from one area to the next.

Business inside the towers had come to a halt. Most of the employees were told they could go home. Some stayed for a while. They were curious to know what had happened. They wanted to see the extent of the damage. Others gratefully left the scene.

*The huge hole caused by the explosion at the World Trade Center reveals several levels of the parking garage below the towers.*

These stunned people were glad to have escaped safely. They looked around to see if their friends were all right. Most of all, people asked each other: What happened?

A chilling answer began to spread among the crowds. Artie Zanfini remembers, "There were rumors of a bomb."[7] Hearing this, people were shocked. They expressed anger, fear, and confusion.

News of the explosion spread throughout the nation. Americans were stunned at the idea of a bombing, especially in such a busy place. People wondered why the World Trade Center had been targeted. The death toll from such a bomb could be enormous. Who would have done such a thing?

Search teams lead search dogs through the streets of New York, as they prepare to head into the underground parking garage.

Members of the New York City Bomb Squad and Federal Bureau of Investigation (FBI) came to inspect the site. Officials from the Port Authority of New York and New Jersey also arrived. The Port Authority owns and operates the World Trade Center.

Members of the bomb squad examined the site of the blast. The bomb had exploded in an underground parking garage below the twin towers. It left a two-hundred-foot-wide crater—about half the size of a football field. Cars

*H*eavy debris litters an elevator lobby in the World Trade Center parking garage after the explosion there.

had been turned into metal shreds. Lt. Walter Boser was the head of the New York Police Department's bomb squad. He showed reporters how the paint had melted off some cars. Boser said the force and intense heat made the paint peel off "like petals of a flower."[8]

Six floors of the underground garage were destroyed. The source of all electrical power inside this vast complex

A government employee displays antiterrorism posters following the bombing of the World Trade Center. A reward was offered for information on the bombers.

was ruined. One employee had probably been killed. Others might also be dead. Rescue workers searched the rubble for bodies.

New York officials called in the FBI. The FBI deals with terrorism, the use of violence for a political purpose. Bombs are often planted by terrorists or terrorist groups. An FBI spokesperson claimed that the FBI would find out who had planted the bomb. This case was now their top priority.

Meanwhile, the police department was receiving calls about the bombing. More than sixty-three calls came in that week. Some people claimed they had planted the bomb. Officials followed up different leads. There was no proof that any of these callers were telling the truth, however. The city of New York offered a reward of one hundred thousand dollars to anyone who could tell them who had set off the bomb.

People also wondered about security. Would the bomber or bombers strike again? Would "copycat" bombers try to imitate this crime? How could people working in other buildings be safe?

Lisa Vasquez was among the people who waited for answers. She told reporter Jim Zarroli, "I want to know who did it and why'd they do it. . . . Why? That's all I want to know. Why us?"[9]

# CHAPTER 3

# An Act of Terrorism

**S**ome of the offices in the World Trade Center reopened about a week after the bombing. Employees returned to work. Many offices still had no heat, however. Some people felt uneasy or fearful about being inside the towers. Lisa Vasquez said, "It's very cold. It doesn't feel safe, to be honest with you."[1]

Numerous businesses moved temporarily to other buildings in New York. The Xerox Business Services' World Trade Center print shop was one of them. The shop had been located on basement level 3. It was severely damaged by the bomb. Repairs would take four months to complete.

It was announced that most of the World Trade Center would be officially closed for at least a month. The heating and air-conditioning systems and fire alarms had to be repaired. Building experts were called in. They checked the steel frame of the towers for damage.

By this time, five people had been found dead as a

result of the bombing. One man was still reported missing. He was thirty-seven-year-old restaurant buyer Wilfredo Mercado. Mercado had been seen unloading supplies in the parking garage around the time of the explosion. It was believed that his body was under the wreckage left by the bomb.

His family continued to hope that Mercado would be found alive. They had come to New York from Peru where earthquakes are not uncommon. There, people are often found alive in the rubble left by quakes. Air spaces in the rubble enable them to breathe until they are rescued.

It took seventeen days to remove the debris left by the bombing. Crews worked to clear out piles that were twelve feet deep. These piles weighed more than one

*W*orld Trade Center employees move computers out of the building following the bombing. The employees were relocated while repairs were made.

*W*orkers clear debris in an underground corridor of the World Trade Center following the bombing.

thousand tons—2 million pounds. The deputy executive director of the Port Authority explained the dangers. He said, "There are enormous hanging slabs of concrete, there are horizontal beams that are not secure, and there is debris falling almost constantly from overhead."[2]

Search dogs were brought in to help locate any bodies. On May 15, officials announced that a man's body had been found. It was Wilfredo Mercado. His family and friends mourned, as did those of the other victims. The

The force of the explosion at the World Trade Center caused enormous damage to the strongly built towers which stand 1,350 feet high.

*W*orkers clear rubble from the underground parking garage at the World Trade Center. A great deal of money will go toward building repairs.

human toll from the bombing was now six deaths and one thousand injuries.

The bomb also took a huge economic toll—about $600 million. Some of this money paid for repairs to the buildings. Millions were also lost when businesses could not operate. Businesses could not produce or sell their goods or services as usual.

While workers began repairing the towers, police looked for the culprits. From the start, they thought more than one person was involved. James Fox was the FBI New York chief. He said, "I think we put the lone bomber, the lone zealot idea on the back burner."[3] The police did not think one person could handle such a large load.

Investigators had some leads. They talked to parking attendants in the garage about the cars that had come inside. Also, a security camera had been operating at one of the three public entries to the garage. Police said they would study the videotape made by that camera. It might contain more clues.

Early in March, police told the public what they had learned. The police said the bomb had exploded on a ramp. This ramp led to the second-underground-level parking garage beneath one of the towers. The bomb was able to release vast energy in this closed-up space. It caused enormous damage to these strongly built towers, which stand 1,350 feet high. The force of the explosion caused walls and floors in the basement to collapse.

Police guessed that the bomb had contained several hundred pounds of explosives. They believed these heavy explosives were brought in a van. The explosive-laden van had been parked beneath the Vista Hotel, located below the towers. Many more people would have died when the bomb went off if the hotel's restaurant had not been empty. More deaths would also have occurred if the van had been parked in a different spot. Thousands might have died if the bomb had exploded around 5:00 P.M., when people were going to their cars to drive home.

Reporters still had many questions. Some asked if the bombers had driven two vehicles inside the garage. Could one vehicle have shifted its load into the other van, then left? Reporters also wondered if any bombers had died in

*A*s police officers examine the debris in the World Trade Center parking garage, rumors of a terrorist attack begin to surface.

the blast. Police said there were no facts to back up this idea.

Soon, there were rumors that the FBI suspected terrorists. Terrorism—the use of violence for a political purpose—has plagued countries around the world for decades. Europe and the Middle East have suffered many terrorist acts. Political terrorism began to rise in the 1960s. Airports and aircraft have often been the focus. In 1988, Arab terrorists targeted a large United States passenger plane. Pan Am Flight 103 exploded as it flew over Lockerbie, Scotland. In 1995, Japanese terrorists used poison gas to attack people in a Tokyo subway.

No large-scale terrorist attacks had occurred before within the United States. However, some terrorists had planned to commit such acts. In 1988, police arrested Yu Kikumura, a Greek-born bookstore owner. Kikumura was caught while driving from New Jersey toward New York City. There, he planned to blow up some large office buildings. Inside his car were three homemade bombs. After his trial, Kikumura was sentenced to a long prison term.

International terrorism is difficult to control. Governments of different countries have discussed ways to cooperate in fighting terrorism. Conventions were held in Tokyo (1963), in The Hague in the Netherlands (1970), and in Montreal (1971). The United Nations hosted conferences on terrorism in 1973 and 1979. In December 1976, European nations held their Convention on Suppression of Terrorism.

The participants agreed on penalties that their nations would enforce for certain crimes. These crimes included hijacking and sabotage of aircraft, hostage taking, and attacking diplomats. Governments also agreed to cooperate with one another to prevent terrorism. They share the information they gather about terrorist groups and their activities.

Now, a major terrorist attack *had* taken place in the United States. The bomb at the World Trade Center had gravely damaged the largest building in New York. It had killed six people and injured hundreds of others.

Law enforcement officials wanted some answers. They studied the parking garage and found traces of

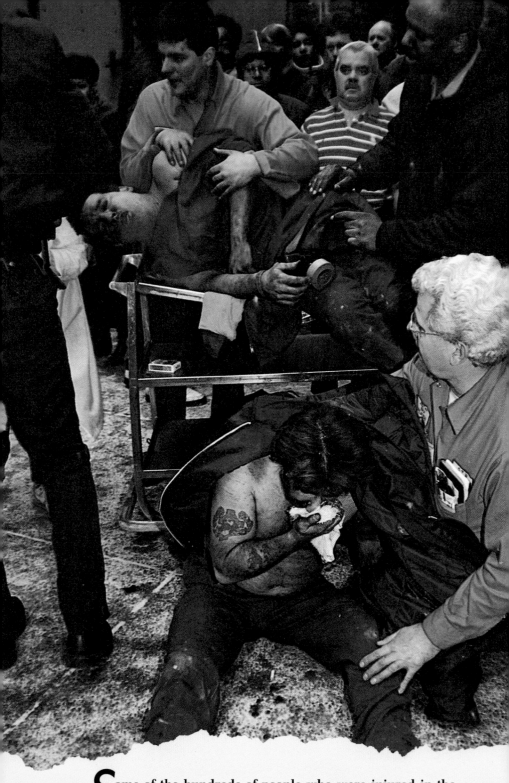

*S*ome of the hundreds of people who were injured in the bombing are shown here following the explosion.

agricultural fertilizer. Such fertilizer can be used to make explosives. Investigators contacted stores in the area that had sold large amounts of this material. Later, they would find that the explosives used in this bombing weighed 1,200 pounds.

Pieces of a yellow Ryder van were found at the bomb site. It seemed that this van had brought the explosives into the parking garage. The FBI contacted Ryder rental agencies until they found the right one. Records showed that a man had rented the van. His name and telephone number were on file. Not only that, the man had returned to the rental agency three times after the bombing. He was trying to get back his deposit, claiming that the truck had been stolen.

The FBI set out to find this man. Just six days after the bombing, they were ready to make an arrest.

# CHAPTER 4

# Brought to Justice

The FBI found the first bombing suspect in Jersey City, New Jersey. Agents said that Mohammed Salameh had planned the bombing. He had rented the van used in the bombing and bought the explosives.

Salameh had been born in Jordan, a Middle Eastern nation. He had entered the United States illegally and found work as a cabdriver. A search of Salameh's apartment turned up suspicious photographs. They showed him with a man who had been convicted of conspiracy in the 1990 murder of a well-known rabbi who lived in New York City.

This man also had connections with other suspected terrorists. One of them was Sheik Omar Abdel-Rahman. The FBI had been investigating Abdel-Rahman for several crimes, including breaking immigration laws. In 1981, Rahman had been accused of issuing an order to assassinate Egyptian president Anwar Sadat. The sheik had also been accused of urging people to overthrow the Egyptian government. Some followers hoped to replace the current government with their own leaders. However, Abdel-Rahman had not been found guilty of these crimes. One American newsman said that Abdel-Rahman's followers looked to him for guidance. They viewed him as "almost a god."[1]

Another suspect was arrested early in March. He was twenty-five-year-old Nidal Ayyad, a chemical engineer from Kuwait. Ayyad was now a United States citizen who lived in New Jersey. The night of the bombing, he had fled to JFK International Airport. He was arrested as he tried to leave the country. The FBI thought Ayyad made the explosives used to bomb the World Trade Center.

A third man, Mah-mud Abouhalima, was arrested in Egypt. He was a German citizen who had been born in Egypt in 1960. Witnesses claimed they had seen Abouhalima with Mohammed Salameh in recent weeks. Abouhalima also had once worked for Sheik Omar Abdel-Rahman. Newsman Jim Zarroli said, "This is the first direct connection between the Sheik and any of the suspects in the bombing."[2]

By the end of March, four men were set to stand trial for the bombing. They were placed in solitary confinement and held without bail. It was the biggest terrorist arrest in United States history.

Assistant Attorney General Gilmore Childers was assigned to prosecute the case. Prosecutors knew they might face an uphill battle in court. There were no eyewitnesses to the bombing. The defendants claimed they were innocent.

However, the prosecution had physical evidence. At the trial, they showed fragments of the van that had carried the bomb. They brought in records from the Ryder rental agency. These records showed who had rented that

*F*ederal agents lead Nidal Ayyad, his head covered with a coat, into federal court.

van. Other records showed who had bought explosives before the bombing. Prosecutors showed letters Ayyad had written, saying he took part in the bombing.

Prosecutors also showed jurors a videotape that belonged to one of the suspects. The video portrayed a simulated (make believe) bombing.

In all, prosecutors presented 1,003 pieces of evidence. They called 207 witnesses. Some witnesses were people who survived the explosion. They recalled stumbling through the ruins and the smoke while trying desperately to escape. One of these witnesses was stock trader Timothy Lang. He had just parked his car in the trade center garage when the bomb exploded. Reporter Jim Zarroli said Lang told the jury he was knocked "dazed and unconscious. Coughing from the smoke, his neck bleeding, he crawled through piles of rubble before collapsing."[3]

Another survivor sobbed on the witness stand. He described how he was standing in his cashier's booth in the garage at the time of the explosion. The booth had crashed around him. Chunks of debris had struck and injured his head.

In the end, two defendants admitted they *had* taken part in the bombing. They claimed the others had forced them into it, however. Only one defendant chose to put on a case of his own. The other attorneys did not present evidence, and their clients did not testify. They said the government had not proved its case beyond a reasonable doubt. They also complained about the testimony from

*A* clock among the wreckage shows the time of the blast at the World Trade Center.

the survivors of the bombing. They said prosecutors were making an unfair "emotional pitch to the jury."[4]

In the end, the jury convicted all four men. None of them begged the court for mercy. Each was sentenced to a total of 240 years in prison with no parole. The number 240 was the remaining life expectancy of all six dead victims, added together.

The government was not finished. A second trial related to the bombing began in January 1995. The FBI had arrested Sheik Abdel-Rahman and eleven other men. They accused these men of terrorism conspiracy in the bombing. An FBI informant had secretly joined this group. He recorded talks in which the group planned to bomb the Lincoln and Holland tunnels and the United Nations Building.

Other evidence revealed plans to destroy United States landmarks. The group's list of future targets included major television stations, other large office buildings in New York City, and the FBI headquarters in Washington, D.C. They also planned to kill certain political leaders. These people included the secretary general of the United

*A*n artist's drawing shows federal judge Kevin Duffy. He questioned possible jurors before the trial.

Nations and New York senator Alphonse D'Amato, among others.

One member of the group agreed to testify against the others. One district attorney said, "You can't in the name of religion commit serious crimes."[5]

The year 1995 brought still more arrests in the World Trade Center bombing. One suspect was charged with driving the van into the garage. The FBI later found the man they believed had organized the bombing plot and arrested him in February 1995.

Law enforcement officials were praised for finding more of the terrorists. Attorney General Janet Reno said that the government wished to send a strong message. She said that when people kill or injure Americans, "no ocean is too wide, no distance too far, no time period too long and no effort too great to make."[6]

# CHAPTER 5

# "I Will Never Forget It"

The trials of the terrorists brought back painful memories for many survivors. There were also many physical reminders of the bombing. A year later, workers were still working to cover the crater in the garage. The hole, about three stories deep, was finally repaired.

Life had to go on. Yet the people who lived through the bombing continued to suffer the physical and emotional effects of the experience. Those who had been badly injured required ongoing medical care. Some people could not return to their jobs for months.

Businesses and their owners and employees continued to suffer. The Vista Hotel was not able to reopen for a whole year. Smoke had also ruined the restaurant at the top of the tower. It was closed for twelve months after the bombing.

A distressing event happened only a few days after some businesses moved back in. The trade center received a bomb threat. This threat proved to be false, but inside

*A*s commuters head for work on the Monday morning after the blast, members of the K-9 police unit patrol the railroad station under the World Trade Center.

the towers, some people felt panic. They feared they would never feel safe again.

Then just a few months after the bombing, the lights at the World Trade Center went off. This time, it was an electrical problem. But the experience terrified some people. They knew what had happened the last time the lights went out. Some people had not realized they were still so upset about the bombing. This experience showed them they had not recovered completely.

The employees of the Xerox Business Services' print shop returned to work in July 1994. Manager Ron Hecht said, "Many people in our work group were anxious."[1] They had to cope with one problem after another. About five hundred construction workers were doing repairs on the floors above and below the shop. There was noise, dust from the construction, and smoke from the welders' drills. In August, a water line burst and caused a flood. The print shop was left with no telephone lines for a week.

Hecht says that it "took a while to readjust."[2] But customers were understanding. The employees did a great job. Some people went for individual or group counseling. They talked about the bombing and tried to deal with their fears.

Survivors also experienced illnesses that often occur when people are under stress. They reported suffering from ulcers and asthma, for example. Many had trouble sleeping during the weeks and months after the bombing. They said they felt anxious and unsafe. These problems were related to the bombing.

Some survivors developed new fears. They refused to fly on airplanes or walk into a parking garage. Others were afraid to ride in elevators. One survivor said, "I will never forget it, not for the rest of my life."[3]

A big change that took place after the bombing was increased security. The cost of security operations at the World Trade Center more than doubled. It now runs about $18 million a year. More cameras and alarms have been

*A*dded security measures were put in place following the bombing at the World Trade Center.

installed. Hundreds of security personnel now guard the building and its stairwells.

Tower officials work to make sure only authorized people come inside the towers. Visitors must check in and receive permission to enter. Once inside, they must wear a sticker on their outer clothing at all times. Employees must show their photo IDs before they are allowed in.

Public parking is no longer permitted in the garages beneath the towers. Now, only tenants in the building may use the underground parking. Delivery trucks and vans are photographed as they arrive. If they look suspicious, security people can put up a heavy steel barrier. This will keep the vehicle out of the lot.

The World Trade Center bombing affected people both inside and outside of New York. Terrorism in the United States was now a reality. Some Americans had experienced it firsthand. Many feared this incident would not be the last. An FBI spokesperson said, "I think the United States has not seen the last of horrendous acts of terrorism with large losses of life."[4]

Many people tried to find something positive to focus on after the tragedy of the bombing. Ron Hecht of Xerox

*T*his car entering Rockefeller Center's parking garage was subject to a strict search following the bombing at the World Trade Center.

said, "There were a lot of heroes on that day a year ago. Now we've had time to put it behind us and move ahead."[5]

Maria Hinojosa, a reporter for National Public Radio, said that one idea comforted many people after the bombing occurred: "The blast proved that the only thing stronger than the towers were the people in them."[6]

# Other Terrorist Attacks

| DATE | DESCRIPTION |
|------|-------------|
| September 5, 1972 | Arab terrorists shoot and kill eleven members of the Israeli Olympic team at the Summer Olympic Games in Munich, Germany. |
| October 23, 1983 | Shiite Muslim suicide bomber kills 241 servicemen in Beirut, Lebanon. |
| October 7, 1985 | Four members of the Palestinian Liberation Organization seize the Italian cruise ship *Achille Lauro* in open seas near Port Said, Egypt. One passenger, an American man, is shot and killed before the hijackers surrender on October 9, 1985. |
| December 1988 | Pan Am Flight 103 is bombed over Lockerbie, Scotland, by Libyan terrorists. Two hundred seventy people are killed. |
| September 1989 | UTA Flight 772 bombed over Niger by Libyan terrorists. One hundred seventy-one people are killed. |
| April 10, 1992 | Irish Republican Army (IRA) claims responsibility for a car bomb that explodes in the London financial district. Three people are killed; ninety-one are injured. |
| March 20, 1995 | Japanese terrorists release sarin, a poisonous nerve gas, in five Tokyo subway cars. Twelve people are killed; fifty-five hundred are injured. Members of the religious cult Aum Shinrikyo later claim responsibility. |
| April 19, 1995 | Japanese terrorists release phosgene, a poisonous gas, in a crowded train in Yokahama, Japan. |
| April 19, 1995 | Alfred P. Murrah Federal Building in Oklahoma City is bombed. One hundred sixty-eight people are killed; hundreds are injured. |
| July 25, 1995 | A bomb explodes in a crowded commuter train in Paris, France. Four people die instantly; eight others are injured, some critically. |
| November 13, 1995 | U.S. Air Force Base military training and communications center in Riyadh, Saudi Arabia, is bombed. Six people are killed. |
| February 25, 1996 | Hamas, a Palestinian terrorist group, bombs an Israeli bus in West Jerusalem. Twenty-four passengers and the bomber are killed. |
| April 18, 1996 | Islamic militants shoot and kill eighteen Greek tourists outside a hotel in Cairo, Egypt. |

26, 199

**Chapter 1.** A Nightmare We All Went Through

1. Author interview with Artie Zanfini, April 19, 1997.

2. Ibid.

3. Interview with Maria Hinojosa, "Some Choose Not to Remember the Bombing," *All Things Considered*, National Public Radio (NPR), February 25, 1994.

4. B. Hewitt, "Trapped in the Towers," *People*, March 15, 1993, p. 80.

5. Interview with Linda Wertheimer, "Investigation Continues in Trade Center Bombing," *All Things Considered*, National Public Radio, March 1, 1993.

**Chapter 2.** Hours of Confusion

1. Author interview with Artie Zanfini, April 19, 1997.

2. Interview with Linda Wertheimer, "Investigation Continues in Trade Center Bombing," *All Things Considered*, National Public Radio, March 1, 1993.

3. Mike Wallace, "The World Trade Center Bombing," *The Twentieth Century*, Arts & Entertainment network, 1996.

4. B. Hewitt, "Trapped in the Towers," *People*, March 15, 1993, p. 81.

5. Ibid.

6. Interview with Maria Hinojosa, "Some Choose Not to Remember the Bombing," *All Things Considered*, National Public Radio, February 25, 1994.

7. Author interview with Artie Zanfini, April 19, 1997.

8. Quoted in United Press International (UPI): "Police Say World Trade Bomb Planted on Parking Garage Ramp," *The New York Times*, March 3, 1993.

9. Interview with Linda Wertheimer, "Investigation Continues."

**Chapter 3.** An Act of Terrorism

1. Interview with Linda Wertheimer, "Investigation Continues in Trade Center Bombing," *All Things Considered*, National Public Radio, March 1, 1993.

2. Interview with Margot Adler, "Final Body Found in WTC Debris," *Morning Edition*, National Public Radio, March 16, 1993.

3. Interview with Linda Wertheimer, "Investigation Continues."

## Chapter 4. Brought to Justice

1. Mike Wallace, "The World Trade Center Bombing," *The Twentieth Century*, Arts & Entertainment network, 1996.

2. "Third Suspect Arrested in Trade Center Bombing," *All Things Considered* with Robert Siegal, National Public Radio, March 24, 1993.

3. "World Trade Center Bombing Trial Has Begun," *Weekend Edition* with David Molphus, National Public Radio, October 9, 1993.

4. Ibid.

5. Mike Wallace, "The World Trade Center Bombing."

6. Quoted in Associated Press (AP) and Reuters News Service report: "World Trade Center Bombing Suspect Pleads Innocent," *Detroit Press*, July 11, 1995.

## Chapter 5. "I Will Never Forget It"

1. Quoted in Xerox Communications, "World Trade Center Bombing: Print Shop Puts Pieces Back Together,"' *Consultant Update*, February 1994.

2. Ibid.

3. Author interview with Artie Zanfini, April 17, 1997.

4. Quoted in Mike Wallace, "The World Trade Center Bombing," *The Twentieth Century*, Arts & Entertainment network, 1996.

5. Quoted in Xerox Communications, "World Trade Center Bombing."

6. Interview with Maria Hinojosa, "Some Choose Not to Remember the Bombing," *All Things Considered*, National Public Radio, February 25, 1994.

asthma—A condition that causes a tight feeling in the chest and difficulty in breathing.

debris—Scattered pieces of something that has broken apart.

hijacking—Seizing control of an airplane, bus, or ship and forcing those in control to do specific things in exchange for their safety.

prosecutor—An attorney representing the public who charges suspects in a crime and tries to prove the case against them in court.

sabotage—The act of damaging an object or process so that it does not function properly.

terrorism—The use of violence or the threat of violence to achieve a political purpose.

ulcer—An inflamed area of the lining of the stomach and intestines.

# Further Reading

## Books

Able, Deborah. *Hate Groups.* Hillside, N.J.: Enslow Publishers, Inc., 1995.

Davis, Lee. *Man-Made Catastrophes.* New York: Facts on File, 1993.

Dobson, Christopher, and Ronald Payne. *Counterattack: The West's Battle Against the Terrorists.* New York: Facts on File, 1982.

Evans, Ernest. *Calling a Truce to Terror: The American Response to Terrorism.* Westport, Conn.: The Greenwood Press, 1997.

Greenberg, Keith, and John Isaac. *Children in Crisis: The Middle East: The Struggle for a Homeland.* Woodbridge, Conn.: Blackbirch Press, 1997.

Hyde, Margaret O., and Elizabeth H. Forsyth. *Terrorism: A Special Kind of Violence.* New York: Dodd, Mead, 1987.

Landau, Elaine. *Terrorism: America's Growing Threat.* New York: Dutton Lodestar, 1992.

Lang, Susan S. *Extremist Groups in America.* New York: Franklin Watts, 1990.

Meltzer, Milton. *The Terrorists.* New York: Harper and Row, 1983.

Raynor, Thomas P. *Terrorism: Past, Present, and Future.* New York: Franklin Watts, 1982.

## Internet Sites

**World Trade Center Bombing**

<http://www.scimitar.com/revolution/multi/terrorism/wtc.html>

**World Trade Center Bombing Trial**

<http://head1.yahoo.com/Full_Coverage/World_Trade_Center_Bombing_ Trial/>